To:

_____

From:

_____

Date:

_____

RORY FEEK

Once Upon the Very First Christmas

Illustrated by
CHRISTINE CUDDIHY

Tommy
NELSON®

An Imprint of Thomas Nelson

Once Upon the Very First Christmas

© 2023 Rory Feek

Tommy Nelson, PO Box 141000, Nashville, TN 37214

Published in Nashville, Tennessee, by Tommy Nelson. Tommy
Nelson is an imprint of Thomas Nelson. Thomas Nelson is a
registered trademark of HarperCollins Christian Publishing, Inc.

Tommy Nelson titles may be purchased in bulk for educational,
business, fundraising, or sales promotional use. For information,
please email SpecialMarkets@ThomasNelson.com.

ISBN 978-1-4002-4701-1 (eBook)
ISBN 978-1-4002-4702-8 (HC)
ISBN 978-1-4002-4703-5 (board book)
ISBN 978-1-4002-4823-0 (B&N signed ed.)

Library of Congress Cataloging-in-Publication Data is on file.

Written by Rory Feek

Illustrated by Christine Cuddihy

Printed in Malaysia

23 24 25 26 27 IMG 6 5 4 3 2 1

Mfr: IMG / Selangor, Malaysia / September 2023 / PO #12194855

To Indiana and all the sweet children at
our one-room schoolhouse. May you always
remember what Christmas is truly about.

Once upon the very first Christmas, a long, long time ago, before there was a Santa Claus or sleigh bells in the snow . . .

a ruler named Caesar sent out a decree
that a census be taken of each town and family.

So Joseph and his wife, Mary, with a child on the way,
made the journey to Bethlehem, where they were to stay.

But the inn was too full. They had nowhere to sleep . . .

except a lowly stable filled with cows and sheep.

So there in the hay, Mary placed her baby boy.

They named the child Jesus. Their hearts filled with joy.

In the fields to some shepherds, an angel appeared . . .

and said, "Do not be afraid, for good news is here!"

"In the city of David, on this very morn,
in the humblest of places, a new King was born."

The wise men from the East, bearing gifts from afar . . .

bowed down to the child beneath a bright star.

Mary held her little Lamb,
who soon the whole world would know,
once upon the very first Christmas,
a long, long time ago.